the garden daughter
POETRY

taylor blayse

The Garden Daughter—Copyright ©2025 by Taylor Blayse
Published by UNITED HOUSE Publishing

All rights reserved. No portion of this book may be reproduced or shared in any form—electronic, printed,
photocopied, recording, or by any information storage and retrieval system, without prior written permission
from the publisher. The use of short quotations is permitted.

ISBN: 978-1-952840-66-1

UNITED HOUSE Publishing
Waterford, Michigan
info@unitedhousepublishing.com
www.unitedhousepublishing.com

Interior design: Talitha McGuinness,
talitha@unitedhousepublishing.com

Author headshot photographer, Faith Moore.

Printed in the United States of America
2025—First Edition
SPECIAL SALES
Most UNITED HOUSE books are available at special quantity discounts when purchased in bulk by corporations, organizations, and special interest groups. For information, please e-mail orders@unitedhousepublishing.com.

the garden daughter

To my parents—

For my childhood, for chasing your dreams, for loving and supporting me as I chase my own.

This book has been and always will be for you.

Pink Houses

I gripped his hand tightly as we walked through the newly cut grass. The fresh smell stirred something in me. Like the earth had been cleansed of all its dead ends and given the chance to grow again. I was just a little girl then. I was filled with wonder by the way the sun danced across the green blades—how each part moved so silently but just loud enough to communicate and move in sync together.

My father and I were walking through the yard of our family's brand-new home. A home that, at the time, I did not realize would be the home we stayed in permanently. The yard was bare, but my dad is the most imaginative person I know. I could see the ideas trickling through the sparkles in his eyes. He was seeing the picture from his mind so clearly.

"And here is where we will put the greenhouses, Taylor," my dad said, peering down at me by his side.

"But Dad, can we have a pink house instead?" my tiny voice replied.

His contagious laugh boomed over the sea of green.

"Not that kind of house, Taylor Ootski" (he used to always call me that). "This house will be different than any you have seen before."

And just like that, the greenhouses were built, and I was changed forever. In the best way.

I started seeing my life through the eyes of the greenhouses at a very young age. I was fascinated by the patience it took to wait for the flowers to bloom and the process of how they went from a seed to the symphony of colors that danced in the breeze every spring. Any time I felt like I was at a low place in life, I spent time in the greenhouses. They reminded me to slow down and take my time. They reminded me to not take life so seriously. They reminded me that most of my problems were not as big as I often made them out to be.

Sitting in the greenhouses and watching nature unfold around me is a very humbling experience. It makes me feel small, but not in the negative way I often say that phrase. Rather, in the way that I realize there are so many things that are bigger than just me—this world is so much bigger than I sometimes think.

In some ways, I feel like I've been writing this book my whole life, starting with the walk with my dad through the brand-new, empty yard. Some of these poems were written when I was a young teenager, and others were written near the final stages of finishing this book. I have learned so much from the garden and the greenhouses, and it has become the lens through which I view everything else. Writing has always been a way to organize my thoughts on paper, to get through difficult times, and to explain to others how I am feeling. This book captures all of those things.

When I was in college, I took several creative writing classes. I was double majoring in music and English, but my emphasis was creative writing. In one of these classes, we were asked to write a nonfiction narrative short story. We could use any form we wanted, and we could write about anything we wanted. It just had to be about us, and it had to have a clear beginning, middle, and ending.

I wrote my story. I titled it "The Garden Daughter." It was ten pages of short stories from my life, all with metaphors relating back to flowers and life in the garden. I wrote it on watercolor paper and painted the pages with flowers and trees and all the things "little me" could remember from her early days spent in the greenhouse. This book is the expansion of that project, as that project is so near and dear to my heart. It was the first piece of writing that made me feel like I could be a writer.

It's a dream I've always cultivated. There's a picture of me at six years old, sitting at my writing desk, writing one of my short stories. I was so small my feet didn't even touch the ground, and I could barely hold my pencil the right way. But I wanted to write, so I sat down and did just that.

If you gain nothing else from this book, I hope you will walk away with the inspiration to find that childhood part of yourself that you may have kept locked away for a long time now. Do the things "little you" would be so proud of. Do the things you've always wanted to do. I think we're the most beautiful and the most confident when we're doing the things God placed on our hearts from the very beginning.

I am so thankful you picked up this book and that you are holding it in your hands. I hope it encourages you to keep going through all of life's trials. I pray that hope will greet you around every bend. That you will open your heart and allow the garden daughter to be your new friend.

Taylor Blayse

plant the garden

The Imperfect Garden: A Prologue

I never asked for a perfect garden,
So why would I pretend that mine is so?
I never expected my flowers to be perfectly aligned–
I never expected them all to grow.

But I put my soul into the little garden
I was given.
I chose to see the good in the imperfections.
Although it is not perfect, it looks well-loved and lived in.

I never asked for a perfect garden,
I asked for one that would portray my humanness.
I wanted art to reflect life,
To be unafraid of any mistakes–for my courage to be planted in it.

I have always been afraid to take up space.

So I let my garden grow wild;
I let it grow out of my mind's tight constraints.

And now, my imperfect garden gives me new eyes.
It strengthens me and shows me
That I am brave enough to step further than just the prologue
of my life.

the garden daughter

the garden daughter

It was August. I remember waking up with the sun, my stomach twisting in knots as I examined the number of bags sprawled out on my bedroom floor. Bags containing everything that would comfort me–things that would bring me back home when I felt too far away. Because that morning as I woke up, I was leaving for college.

I remember the drive to my beautiful campus. An hour and a half of scenic Missouri roads. Roads that were winding, lined with green trees on either side, roads that reminded me I need only follow them to find my way back home. My dorm room was the size of a closet, my roommate a complete stranger. But I carried the pieces of home with me, and I decorated my room in their bright colors and second-hand warmth. I could do it, I knew that much. I knew it would not be easy. But oftentimes the best things are not.

College was very challenging for me, but it was crucial to my growth as a person. It was exactly what I needed at the time. Though I often felt alone, I simultaneously met some of the most incredible people and finally found my voice. I was encouraged by professors to keep writing, that I had a voice worth sharing, that publishing a book was something they wanted for me.

Flash forward to a cold, December day. I am wearing a cap and gown, sitting in a row of chairs with fellow classmates. As I sat in that metal chair, listening to the professors speak on behalf of graduation, I was bewildered at the way time flies but the way it takes its time all at once. College was long, beautiful, and difficult; but it also flew by in an instant. And here I was, accepting my diploma, realizing that I was beginning all over again. Realizing that a new chapter was about to start, a new season was about to come forth, a new book was about to be written. And I was terrified and elated, knowing that I had no idea what the next

the garden daughter

thing was going to look like. It was scary, but I also saw a field of endless possibilities. And as I look back on that moment now, I am happy I gave myself space to feel that hope– that excitement for something new. Because what I have experienced since that moment has been more than I could have imagined or dreamed.

A seed is the symbol of a fresh start in the garden. It is the indicator that we are moving into a new season, but we will have to start again with our tiny seeds. Many of these poems reflect small beginnings, new things, and new discoveries. There is much written that reveals who I used to be and what God has been teaching me as I have grown older and continued my journey. There are poems that I wrote when I was fifteen, and there are others that were written when I was twenty-two or twenty-three.

I like to remind myself that it is never too late to start over–it is never too late to run to God and accept the plans He has for your life. In the greenhouses, new seeds are planted every winter and make their appearance each spring. Remember this.

You can start new, and you can bloom again. But remember that this process takes time. Seeds are planted, but they do not bloom until they are meant to–until the weather is ready–until they are strong enough–until they have learned all the things they were meant to learn while they were deep in the soil.

I hope these poems remind you of these things. I hope they embody the beauty in small beginnings, the beauty of patience, the beauty of the slow process of time that makes us wiser as it marches on. Most of all, I hope you are inspired to plant new seeds in your life or revisit and nurture some old ones.

Start With a Seed

Long seasons of waiting
Have started to remind me of the flowers
Waiting
To Bloom.

It's a season much like a garden,
Which is beautiful
Too.

Perhaps that's why I love
The garden.
Perhaps that's why the story
Starts there.

Any gardener understands the joy
That comes from finally seeing
Small sprouts that will eventually grow
Tall
And bloom.

And while the flowers,
In all their glory,
Are beautiful,
I can't help but be humbled by the
Little sprouts
That sometimes bring me more joy
Than the flowers do.

And when I look at my life,

the garden daughter

I see new things being born
From a season where I spent so long
Waiting.

And though the flowers certainly aren't in bloom yet,
I'll wait with joy and
Excitement
As I watch the sprouts begin to pop through
The soil.

I have learned to celebrate the tiny
Victories.
The little things that bring me one step closer
To where I want to be.

I encourage you to
Celebrate it all,
Big and small.
And remember that the flowers will bloom
Soon.

But in the meantime,
Sit and marvel at the little
Sprouts.

Growing a garden is no small feat.
Becoming who you want to be is no small feat too.

Memento
Love for an instrument far overlooked

My marimba's deep resonance seeps strongly into my bones.
A yarn mallet, an extension of my arm,
Controlling every magical moment,
Creating a melody all my own.

And this piece, titled Memento
Tugs tightly at my heart.
The pitch of the deep wooden bars
Rattling my chest,
Matching the sweetness of this new start.

This instrument and I,
We become one.
I learn the gaps between the bars,
Muscle memory taking my arms
There.
Chords echo in that small practice room,
Reaching the restricting walls, aching,
Longing
To be shared.

The window of that room,
A backdrop of college campus life,
Of leaves falling,
Umbrellas opening,
Nature pouring forth all it has held so tight.

But my marimba and me,

the garden daughter

We watch from the inside.
Our peaceful, quiet haven.
This quaint practice room.

I will hold this memento in my pocket forever.

This instrument's voice gives life to my own.

One day, we will step outside and perform our dance together.
We will add subtle sweetness to a world of chaos and noise.

My Father's Garden

I see Your love in the garden.
I see my life surrounded by flowers
And colors.
A swirl of emotions
And Your warm embrace.

When I picture being loved freely by You,
I imagine being in your garden.

I imagine Your hand,
Outstretched
Toward
    me.

I imagine You asking if I want to dance.
Not only in that moment,
But for the rest of my life.

When I think of the flowers in my father's garden,
I remember how astounded
I am
By their beauty.

But more than that,
I am in awe of the man
Behind the garden.

I watch him year-round as he cares
So delicately

the garden daughter

For his flowers.
He thinks about them all the time,
Even in the winter months.

When spring makes her first appearance,
My father has already taken great care
Of his small sprouts.

As rough as his hands may be,
They are gentle in that they nurture
Even the most delicate
Seeds.

He pours every ounce of his love into his flowers.

His greenhouses are wide and expansive,
But he has specially prepared
Every inch of them
For each of his unique plants.

He knows exactly where they need to be.
He cares for them
There.

When I think of these things,
I cannot help but wonder
How much greater Your
Love
Is
For
    us.

the garden daughter

You planted us into this short period of time
For a special
Purpose.

For such a time as this.

Because it's true that our time here on earth
Is as fleeting as spring.
We bloom in our time,
And we wither like the flowers.

But like the gardener I know and love,
You care for us
All the seasons
Through.

Doors

When I look back at the life I used to
Grieve,
I feel the absence of that old sense of
Longing.

It felt heavy at first.

"How can I be so okay with this drastic
Turn of events?"
I used to think.

Now, however,
My thoughts are met with,
"How was I so okay
With where I
Used to be?"

Life is messy and hard,
And this part has been full of difficult
Learning.
But there is something so beautiful about this part
Of the journey.

This door I have found myself
Walking through
Is the most unexpected,
But the most
Inviting.

the garden daughter

As I grow,
My next steps feel more
Unclear.

The details are muddled,
The path
Dense.
But I can't help but love this chapter best.

I am proud of how far I have come.

My heart no longer aches
On rainy days,
Or when certain songs play,
Or when certain scents tickle
My nose.

The past is there to help us grow
And to remind us
That goodness is never
Far away.

But we do not belong there anymore.

We belong here,
Now.
Present.

Happiness is found here.

the garden daughter

Some doors open unexpectedly.
I know this one has.

But it has by far been
My favorite.
Here's to letting go
And taking the
Leap
To walk through every door
He opens for me.

No matter how scary
It may
Be.

An Unexpected Friend

Since I was a little girl,
I have had the same enemy.

This enemy often holds me back,
Makes me second-guess,
And grips my hand tightly.

I had always felt powerless
When I felt the presence
Of this enemy.

He came at the worst times–
When I was lonely,
When I was tired,
When I wasn't who
I wanted to be.

Anxiety and I
Grew unfortunately close
As the years passed.

He knows me well,
And I was certain
Our relationship
Would forever last.

Until one day,
The grip on my hand changed.

the garden daughter

It no longer hurt–
It no longer felt
The same way.

A friend of mine was hurting,
And I could see in their eyes,
A familiar,
Deep pain.

I could see their struggle
To escape,
But they could not break
Free
From the chains.

I felt my enemy
Start to occupy my mind.

But as I turned to where
Anxiety once was,
Now instead,
Empathy
Was by my side.

Its face reminded me of my enemy,
But he was now
Clothed in light.

He wore a new smile,
One that said,
"Everything will be alright."

So I turned to my friend
Who was fighting
Their enemy,

And I sat with them
And held their hand,
Just like my new friend
Empathy.

And I thanked God in that moment
For every struggle
And every battle with my mind,

Because if I had not walked
With my enemy,
I would not be comforting
This friend of mine.

So when I feel my enemy
Anxiety
Far too close and always
Nearby,

I remind myself of this:
My new friend
Empathy
Is never too far behind.

Weeds

If you have ever
Been asked
To pull weeds,
You understand what a lousy task
It can be.

It is almost always
Too hot outside to even function properly,
And the weeds are almost always
In areas
Nearly impossible
To reach.

My brothers and I
Spent hours upon hours during our childhood
Pulling weeds from the cracks in our patios.

Down on our hands and knees,
Gloves on,
Sweat dripping,
The weeds so
Tangled,
The job felt nothing less than
Never-ending.

"Every other kid in our grade
Is at the waterpark right now,"
We would say,
Half-heartedly tossing a weed

the garden daughter

Into the pile.
"But no,
Here I am,
Pulling weeds."

Mason would add his two cents in,
Commenting that,
"It just isn't fair.
Why do we need to pull them anyway?
The patios all look fine with them there."

I continued to uproot
The small weeds
From the imperfections
In the concrete.
A seemingly impossible place
For a plant to grow,
And yet,
The weeds seemed happy as
Could be.

Down on the ground,
Meeting eye-to-eye with each plant,
It's funny how only now
I realize
The lesson the weeds
Were so desperately
Trying
To teach me.

God works through

the garden daughter

His world
If you let Him.

My brothers and I
Denied Him the opportunity
To humble us
That day.

Maybe someday I'll understand
How.

How to see the beauty of the things
Right in front of me.

And maybe someday,
I'll tell Him
How much that moment means to me now.

New Seeds

Sometimes,
We do not understand
Why people in our life
Choose to leave.

Sometimes,
We do not understand
Why they could not be
All they had promised
To be.

And we let these thoughts
Engulf our minds.

We let them consume us so much—
We give them more authority than we realize.

We look in the mirror
And blame the face
Staring back at us.

We begin to question whether or not
It was our fault.
Whether or not we did something wrong.

But we are only looking
At fear.

I think fear sometimes screams so loud,

the garden daughter

It makes us forget
We are companions
With courage.

Because courage gently
Whispers to us
In the midst of the shouting,
Reminding us
That we can do it.
When people leave,
We are met with a blank page;
The stomping grounds of starting over.

But we often forget
That bravery holds our hands,
And asks us to start this new path
A little bit bolder.

Sometimes,
We do not understand
Why people in our life
Choose to leave.

But God knows there is a reason.
He knows what must be taken away
In order to fully begin
This new journey.

I hope you'll hold the hand
Of courage–
I hope you'll welcome change

As a new friend.

I hope you'll plant new seeds
In your garden–
I hope you'll see that where one thing ends,
A new one will always
Begin.

Heavy

I love words.

I love the way they dance on the page.

The way they beckon us to stay,
The way they hold us
Tight
In a creative
Embrace.

I love the lighter words.
The happy,
Sad,
Okay.
They float in the air and are quickly
Erased.

But I think of all the words
I love,
It's the heavy words I love
Most.

Like grief,
Change,
Vulnerability,
Hope.

These words linger.
They sink deeper into the soul.

They aren't as flimsy as
Those lighter words.
They grab onto us
And hold.

Because when asked,
"How are you doing today?"
It would be much simpler
To say,
"Oh, I'm doing okay."

But true connection is felt
When we answer the real
And honest way.

What if instead, I said,
"Today, I haven't felt brave.
And I am afraid because
So much
Has changed."

Suddenly,
The questioner becomes
The intent
Listener
Who pulls us out of that trap:

    Our
        minds.

I think I'll keep using

the garden daughter

The heavy words.

They're the words that set us free,

Despite how heavy
They may be.

Quiet

Silence is everything.
We can't have music without silence.
Because the most beautiful and breathtaking part
Of any piece
Is the silence
In-between the notes
On the page.

People are that way, too.

We live in a world of shouting.
The outgoing are pleasurable,
While the quiet ones are asked,
"Why don't you talk?"

They are called "shy" and "awkward."
But really,
You just don't know them.
You don't understand their minds.

So here's to the reserved individuals
Who wonder what they ever did wrong.
"Why am I not like everyone else?"
Is a question constantly racking
Their brains.

No, listen.

We need you.
Your silence fills the gaps between
The notes on
The page.
You make the music of this world
Worth listening to.

Don't ever forget that.

the garden daughter

Digging for Words

We move across time
And place
Digging for the right words to say.

And with each passing moment,
New words start to surface.

Words we weren't wise enough
To understand
A few minutes ago,
A few years ago,
A few decades ago.

Every experience adds to our vocabulary.
Every experience is an opportunity
To learn the words
That will one day help someone else
Who's going through
The same thing.

We spend our whole lives searching for words.
And sometimes when we've found them,
We're too afraid
To say them.

Don't be.

You are right here in this moment for an important reason.

The words you have in your head,
And the vocabulary you've spent so many years expanding—
They exist so another soul may hear them
And be healed.

Memories

What am I supposed to do
When the memories come knocking
Because they're looking
For you?

And I tell them to go away,
To leave this address alone.

To find a new place to reside;
They are not welcome here
Anymore.

But they persist
Like time moving forward,
Like tide coming in.

They knock on wooden doors,
Ring the bells,
Peek through windows,
Aching to revisit.

At first,
I hide.
I push them aside.

But their endless
Pestering
Opens my eyes.

So I let them in.
I dine with them,

the garden daughter

Until they finally feel ready to say
Goodbye.
They leave,
Satisfied.
And wisdom welcomes itself
Into my home instead.

Wisdoms brings new memories.
Ones I cherish.
Ones that keep my heart
From wandering too far off.

Ones that hold the power to put those old memories to rest.

the garden daughter

Found Love

Yes, I found love.

Even after
You.
I found it in places
Where I had forgotten
It existed.

I found it in my parents.
In the way they talked me through
Every tear-filled moment.
In the way their words
Destroyed every
Demon
Inside my head.

I found it in my friends.
The ones who pulled me out
Of those dark places.
The ones who taught me how
To smile again.

I found it in an unexpected soulmate
Who opened so many of my
Locked doors.
Who made me
Braver,
Happier,
Wiser,
Than I had ever felt
Before.

Yes, I found love.

the garden daughter

Know this:
When your heart is broken,
Don't forget to turn
Around.

Because where one person
Walked away,
You will find there are a hundred
Hearts
Waiting to catch you.

And it is those hearts that remind
You
Of what love is all
About.

So yes,
I found love.
I found it in places
Where I had forgotten
It existed.

And because of this found love,
I am grateful for every
Heartbreak.
I am grateful that each closed
Door
Lets me see the hundred
Open ones.

Yes, I found love.
And I have a feeling I will continue to find it
For the rest
Of my
Life.

the garden daughter

To the Earthworm's Work
And to all the flowers you've grown without knowing it

Uprooting weeds,
Taking mud and soil with me.
My purple glove
A splash of lilac against the
Brown dirt and dull, green leaves.

A place where new color is to be planted;
A place specially prepared for rebirth.
A soft space for my soul to land,
For my eyes to wander,
For my feet to feel the soft crevices of earth.

And in my glove, too,
A wiggling thing,
Frantically searching for solitude deep within soil.
An earthworm,
Just beginning his day's work.
A job that is too often disregarded.

Little does he know of the weight his job holds.
For if he were not toiling underneath the dirt–
Preparing it and making it good–
My summer blooms would not shine as they do.
They would not be so daring,
So bold.

Your hard work does not go unnoticed.

There are meadows of wildflowers planted into souls,
All because you were there to hold them
When they needed it most.

You may not always see the fruits of your labor,
The flowers you worked so hard to grow.
But I promise you, like the earthworm,
You leave beauty trailing behind you
Everywhere
You go.

the garden daughter

the garden daughter

annual

the garden daughter

I thought I would be married at twenty-two. I thought a lot of things back then.

The first experience I ever had with heartbreak was in college. A couple of days after my breakup, my dad was very hard on me. I was sitting at the kitchen table of my parents' house, where I had just moved back in because this breakup had forced me to leave my college town. I couldn't stand the sight of the city he and I shared, the places we had visited, the memories we had made. Years and years worth of pictures and stories. How was I supposed to let it all go?

As I was sitting there at the table, sobbing into my plate of scrambled eggs and toast, my dad entered the room. He looked at me and said, "I'm tired of this. I want to see Taylor again. You have too many things going for you—you are too smart and too full of life to let this consume you." And I am not kidding when I say I absolutely did not want to hear anything he was saying to me at that moment. In fact, I despised it.

I felt stripped of my identity because I had put all of mine into another person. I now know, several years later, that we cannot find our worth in any person on this earth. Because they are human and are equally broken. They will, whether they intend to or not, hurt us in some way or another.

As the months continued on, the screams of my sorrow subsided as hope and reason and realization began to speak louder and more confidently to me instead. And I love my dad for what he said, because he opened the door for those new thoughts and new friends.

I began rebuilding myself. Who was I without this person? Who was I before them? Who would I be after? These questions echoed through my brain most days, pestering me to dig deeper into myself to find their answers.

the garden daughter

And as months and years passed by, I found answers in ways I never expected. I found answers in people, in places, in new experiences. But the road there was long, dark, and winding. These poems were written during that trek through the wilderness--that journey through the tangled mess in my heart and the jumbled thoughts and unanswered questions in my mind.

    These poems are sadder than the rest, and to me, they reflect an annual flower. Annuals flower for one season and do not come back the next. They often bloom through the fall and then die with wintry temperatures. These poems show my digging and searching and rediscovering who I could still be. During this time, God's answer had been no. I struggled with this. I had a plan for my life--why was it not working out the way I had hoped and prayed it would?

    I learned a lot about trusting God and what that looks like. He taught me that what He has for me is always better, but I had to go through the hurt first before I could learn that truth.

    Annual flowers are beautiful, but they cannot withstand the freezing cold. During this time of my life, I too felt as though I was not strong enough to make it through the winter. I too longed for summer, longed for sunshine, longed for warmth. But underneath all of that weakness was my friend, Hope--and though these poems are sad, I think you will find that Hope is written between the lines. The annuals have helped me realize that vibrant colors and abundant life can bloom from some of our saddest chapters and our roughest beginnings.

Vinca

I asked God to give purpose
And beauty
To my life.

But gardens aren't beautiful until they've felt the rain.
Until they've lived under the storm clouds
For a while.

And gardens grow weeds.
A term tossed around
So negatively
But one containing much more than we might originally
Think.

Weeds are viewed as annoying conquerors.
Pesky things
That overtake the beauty
Of our gardens.

But what if I reminded you
That some of the most beautiful flowers
Can be considered weeds?
Dandelions, forget-me-nots, vincas.
Yes, even these.

Because the term "weed" is not the definition of the flower,
But the definition of the location
In which it is
Growing.

the garden daughter

Yes, gardens grow weeds.
They multiply and they consume the beauty
One had intended to be there.

But over and over again,
I am reminded
That God loved the weeds so much
That He decided to make flowers out of them.
He has a tendency to take the ugly
And make it
Beautiful.

And the rain comes.
Some days it sprinkles
And others it pours.
But I am reminded by the flowers that
What we think is drowning us
Is actually breathing
Life
Into us.

I am reminded to be thankful
For the rainy seasons.
I am reminded that the sun shines on the other side.
I am reminded that the only possible outcome of the rain
Is to grow
And eventually
Bloom.

In each season,
He meets us where we are.

the garden daughter

He holds us during the storm
And He makes beauty out of the weeds.

Yes, I asked God to give purpose
And beauty
To my life.

And He showed me the beauty in the
Growing season.
The beauty in the
"Not knowing" season.
The beauty in the
Waiting and the weeds.

The beauty in who He is.
Because no matter the circumstances,
He is still good.

So, I'll take a step into the rain.
Let it remind me
That not all gloomy days
Are bad.

The Girl in the Willow

The girl in the willow was a dreamer.

Climbing as high as she could go,
She memorized every nook
And cranny
Of that beautiful and old tree.

The girl in the willow was excited
For all that life
Could and would be.

When she reached the peak and broke through the treetops,
Her heart was elated at the abundant land—
Adventure
And opportunity
Spread out
Before her.

The girl in the willow danced with the wind when it came.

Descending from the shaking branches,
She grabbed hold of its vines,
Immersing herself into the jungle of the tree.

She took its hand and accepted its offer to dance,
Because
Even the things that move to destroy us
Can be embraced
With a heart ready

the garden daughter

To overcome.

The girl in the willow never wanted to leave.

But change comes as quickly as the wind,
And beauty is as fleeting
As spring.

However, that girl knew there was beauty to behold,
And life yet to live,
On the other side
Of the willow tree.

That girl is you,
It's her,
She's me.

the garden daughter

Marigolds–October's Birth Flower

The air starts to cool
And my spirits drop with it.

I see the sunshine fading
Faster and faster–
I wish I could hold it
Longer.
Just for a
Little bit.

I always feel less
Like myself
When the air is cold.

I step outside,
And it takes my breath away
In the worst way.

But then I remember
That cooler weather
Is met with
October.

And then I think
Of marigolds
And their
Vibrant and bright
Colors.

the garden daughter

Suddenly,
The cooler weather
Is not as bad
As it once seemed.

And the depression
That comes with it
No longer has control of me.

But there are still off-days,
Reminding me to never take
The good days
For granted.

And the marigolds,
They show me
That peace can still bloom,
Even where grief
Was planted.

At the Beach

I sit,
Toes curled in the sand,
Eyes lost in the dancing waves
Reaching
Earnestly for me.

What is this powerful,
Mysterious,
Unexplored body of water
Trying to say?

It crashes steadily,
Mimicking
My thundering heart,
Grazing my feet at times and
Engulfing my entire body the next.

But nevertheless, always finding me.
No matter how far back I may sit, no matter
How deeply I bury my toes within the sand,
Hiding in darkness,
Afraid of its touch.

Hope always finds me.

Perhaps she is not so quiet, so timid
As I often think.

No, she persists vigorously,

the garden daughter

Like deep blue waves with white caps
Weary from traveling, but
Strong enough
To venture to shore undoubtedly.

So I sit,
Relishing the feeling of sand,
Its coarseness therapeutic.

I let the waves reach
Me, I let them embrace me tightly.

I let them turn my heart to Hope, her presence
Pairing
With His earnest and unfailing love.
A melody,
A battle,
A dance for my attention.

I let them have it,
I let them hold me,
Here,
At the beach.

the garden daughter

A Winter Song

There is a type of hush about the world when it is wrapped in winter snow.
A white, sparkling blanket taken out of storage.
Dusted off, fanned out,
Tucked in at every crevice of the earth.

I sit at my piano,
My fingers frozen.
In fear or from cold? I do not know.

Suddenly, I notice something new sprawling across the ivories:
A beam of summer light.
I stretch my fingers, reaching for it.
My piano sings in response.

It is timid at first, that winter song.
Quiet, like snowflakes falling.
Like the soft crunch of snow boots trekking through this shimmering terrain.

I let my feet dance along the pedals.
I let them pause with my hands.
I breathe.

And it is here where I notice this:
Music would not be music without silence.
Without the breath of the musician;
Without the space between the notes on the page.

Though the winter may be bleak,
I think of that summer sun beam.
How it thawed my hands, my fear, my heart.
I let that be my song.

Moon Glow

A warm glow embraces the earth as the sun stretches its
golden light.
Sinking into the horizon, kissing
Deep blue waters as it says goodnight.

Bidding farewell as the moon awakens and takes her shift.

The rippling of the waves
Dance to an unheard melody,
Eyes
Poised to the wind, their conductor.
A song only the ear of nature can hear,
A performance
Only the quiet observers might see.

And this rotation, this ever-present
Cycle, undisrupted.
It reminds me that life moves forward, that time goes on,
Even when I would rather it pause for a moment.

But I too must keep going.

The sun still sleeps and rises again
Consistently, despite my emotions that weigh
Heavy
In my heart.
Like the full moon looming above me.

So I grip Grief's hand tightly and we
Traverse this world together,
Catching sun rays and bottling them up for our weary souls,
A kind of magic I wish to hold

Onto.

We pocket silver moonlight as it
Shimmers
Lightly
On tallest treetops,
Revealing a different kind of joy we long to savor.

Light still lives here.

My life keeps going, even when I want it to slow down or pause.
The moon awakens as darkness falls,
But
It still shines its luminescence on my heart.

Zinnia

There is no escape
From pain,
There is only
Strength.

There is only the choice
To get up
And keep going,
Even on the gloomiest of
Days.

I feel the lack of the
Sun
In the cold winter months.

I feel the deep,
Gray sky–
The faded colors sink deeply
Into my bones.

It has a tendency to
Wipe out
Everything I have learned
About hope.

I must remind myself
I am only missing
The sun.
And that life won't be like this forever–
I must just
Wait patiently
For the summer months.

the garden daughter

God holds me tight
When I feel a little weaker.
He holds me tight
In the midst of the days
That look
Bleaker.

But I am reminded of
The zinnia,
Of its rainbow
Assorted petals;
Its unique set
Of sunshine colors.

I am reminded that
A zinnia
Requires full sun
To remain colorful and
Strong.

So I will hold on
Until then.
I will remember that,
With hope,
Winter is never
Too long.

the garden daughter

Squirrels and College Campuses

Shades of red,
Orange, and
Yellow
Embrace the outer edges of my once green trees.
Their final explosion of color before their
Goodnight,
Their serendipitous slumber.

Squirrels scurry across leaf-laden sidewalks,
Hurrying from one home to the next,
Their warm eyes and twitching noses
Making contact with me for just a moment.

My sneakers meet
Smooth pavement, my
Heart clenching
At every gentle crunch of leaves
Beneath my feet.

Whether this feeling reflects mourning
My summer,
Or anticipating the start of fall,
I do not know.

But it is autumn,
And college has started,
And I can't express how I feel about anything
With certainty anymore.

The brick music building meets the
Skyline of my sight.
A familiar feeling washes over me,
Adjacent to peace.

Maybe I have found some sense of solace
In the ever-changing nature of things.

A Traveler Leaves–I am Left with Memories

I wonder what will go through
His head
When he boards the first plane.

I wonder if he'll smile,
Knowing he did
The brave thing.

Knowing that he is on his way.

I wonder if his stomach will twist in
Knots
From the looming cloud of
Second-thoughts and
"Should-I-even-be-leaving?"

I wonder if he'll shed a tear,
Knowing he is leaving everything behind
For a short time.

I wonder if he'll think of us–
If he'll think of me.

When people leave and begin a new chapter without me,
I feel like I am being left
Behind.

I feel inclined
To start a new chapter
Too,
But the reality is that I am living in a different
Book.

I am reading at a different pace.

And while his chapter here is ending,
Mine continues on.

The only difference is that one of my favorite characters
Is departing.

When people leave,
All the memories seem to come flooding
Back.
Images pop into my head,
Old conversations fill my ears,
And warm emotions
From the best days
Fill my chest
With peace.

I try to capture these memories in my head,
But each is met with tears rolling down my cheeks.

I am so happy for what he will see.
But I am not, and never will be
Prepared
For him
To leave.

Geraniums & Greenhouses

Every year,
When I walk into the greenhouses
Through that familiar
Wooden door,

I admire how they are so different
Yet somehow just as beautiful
As the year before.

I notice how my breath
Catches
For a moment;
How my heartbeat
Seems to slow.

I am wrapped in a familiar
Feeling,
As peace rushes and
Dances and
Magnificently overflows.

My eyes catch the geraniums first.

They are planted in
Lovely hanging baskets,
Bringing the greenhouses
So much more
Life.

And I remember how they're here
Every year,
In ways that may be
Different
From last time.

the garden daughter

Because the truth is that a greenhouse
Never looks the same
Each new spring.
Yes,
Some of the flowers remain,
But there is new beauty to behold–
New beauty the new season brings.

And I feel we all
Are a greenhouse
Of our own.

We change,
We bloom,
We prune,
In more ways than
We often know.

I will never have who I am now,
So I will love her even in her
Weaknesses and
Insecurities.

I will never have who I am now,
So I will love her no matter what
Each new season
Brings.

To All The Pictures We Never Took

You ask me why
I love pictures
So much.

Why I need to hold the memories
In my hands–
Why I need to feel their touch.

You ask me why
I feel the need to capture
Every moment
Rather than living in it.

Why I can't just
Be content with my surroundings–
Why you think I am less
Content
Than I wish to admit.

But I would tell you
That our brains are just not capable
Of remembering people
Exactly as they once were.

The details get muddled,
Their smile fades from our mind.

And here I find myself,
Late at night,
Alone.

Wishing there were people
I could reach out to–
People I used
To know.

But where do I find my comfort now?

In the photographs you spent
So much time
Criticizing.

As I flip through
The old pictures,
My mind shifts from
Sorrow to
Realization.

I reminisce on my friends
And family
As they once were.

The memories are
As clear as a new piece of
Paper–
They are no longer a blur.

And little by little,
I am remembering who
I used to be.

I am remembering who
I can still become–
The person that
I
    Need.

I am remembering the
Light
That was once in my eyes.

The passion in my heart–
The excitement in my

the garden daughter

Everyday life.

It was a flame
That you blew out
Slowly and steadily
Over the course of the
Years.

And I find myself wishing
That the thought of you
Had not wasted
So many
Of my tears.

You made me wish
Myself
Out of existence.

You made me wish
That I could be
Someone different.

Someone who would be
Better suited
For you.

But that version of me
Was simply not
True.

And now that your wind is gone,
I am left with the ashes
Of who I once
Was.

And I am left pondering
Just how much damage

the garden daughter

One soul could
Cause.

But I will keep taking
Photographs,
For they bring my heart
Great joy.

I will keep documenting
My life–
I will keep smiling at the things
I enjoy.

I will rekindle the flame
Of who I once was
Before you came along.

I will reignite what makes
Me,
Me.

Before things went
So horribly
Wrong.

Winter Roads

I come to a dip
In the road.
I'm driving alongside
That valley now.

One of the most beautiful
I've ever known.

I love this road
At golden hour.
I love the way the light
Trickles through the leaves.

The way summer green
Stretches wide like my beloved blue seas.

The world is blanketed
In that golden,
Green glow.

My sunroof is open,
My skin is sun-kissed,
And my freckles are starting
To show.

And I am reminded
That beautiful things
Come back to us
In ways we may not
Expect.

And sometimes,
The very things that
Bring them near
Are things we so often

the garden daughter

Neglect.

Because the truth
Is that I despise the winter cold.

But without it,
I would not love summer
So much.

I would not appreciate
The way it gives us every color
All at once.

I would not appreciate
Its warmth,
Its sunshine,
Its way of making us
Fall in love.

No,
I would not appreciate
These things
About the season that holds
My heart.

No,
I would not appreciate them
If it were not for
Winter.

For the way it forces me
To refocus—
To stop and
Restart.

the garden daughter

Sunflowers

When I was a little girl,
I asked my father to plant
A sunflower circle.

I wanted a reading nook.
A place to escape with a good book.

And he did so, with a smile
On his face.
He mapped it all out
And showed me
Each day.

I watched the sunflowers grow
Tall and strong.
I watched as they turned their beautiful,
Golden faces to the sun.

And as they grew,
I grew,
Too.

And when that sunflower forest
Finally emerged,
I spent hours and hours
Curled up within the stems
Reading my favorite books.

I am older now,
And the sunflowers have long since
Passed away.
But that little girl lives on
Deep within
Where the sunflowers
Once stayed.

the garden daughter

The words from her books
Still linger
There.

Like whispers in a gentle spring breeze.

And when she forgets
The warm days
And the flowers in her
Hair,

She realizes
All she must do to remember
That old love—

Yes, like the sunflowers,
All she must do
Is turn her face
Toward the sun.

the garden daughter

the garden daughter

grow

the garden daughter

the garden daughter

About six months after I had crawled out of that dark hole and started to find myself again, I saw an opening for a job as a middle- and high-school English teacher at a local Christian school. I had known about this school for years, but I had never attended or even visited. But I felt God tug at my heart, urging me to take the leap. So I called the number and explained that I was interested in the position. I interviewed and got the job the next week.

This job was one of the biggest turning points in my life, and I cannot write this book without telling you about my amazing students. They are my biggest encouragers–the ones who inspire me the most. Their kind hearts and warm souls were exactly what mine needed. And as I met them and taught them and got to know them, I don't think they realized just how much they impacted and led to my healing.

I grew so much as a person when I became a teacher. I am a quiet person at heart, and being an educator threw me way outside of my comfort zone in all the ways God knew I needed to be. I would not be the person I am today if I had not experienced that job for two years. I don't even think I would be writing this book if my students hadn't been so encouraging and excited for me throughout the entire process. Teaching was a time in my life where I felt like God had answered all of my questions from that dark place. I met some incredible people through this job. I made friends that became more than just "coworkers". These wonderful people truly became mentors and even family; because not only did I make so many new friends, but I met my future husband too. And when I look back on those days, I look back on them so fondly.

I love writing about growth and new realizations as we get older and uncover so many answers to our questions. These poems reflect the times when things started making sense to me. This is where I started to see God's plan unfolding. These poems represent the time of my life when I felt like the most personal growth happened in a very short amount of time. I felt as though I was learning new things constantly. God was showing me His plan for my life, and everything was starting to make sense again.

This time of my life opened my eyes to how much

the garden daughter

I truly appreciated the "annuals" in my life–how much I valued and still do relish the beautiful things that had "died." I learned that some really great things must end in order for God to show me all of the even greater, more colorful, and brighter things He has for me.

I hope these poems inspire you to never stop growing, to never stop learning, and to never stop paying close attention to everything God has done and continues to do in your life. His plan truly is best, and I loved getting to live this season of growth with Him by my side. I felt like He kept telling me, "Just hang on, this is the part where the story gets good." And as I held onto Him tightly, I saw just how true that was. I saw just how much He was helping me grow.

Home

"People are not homes,"
I read.

But what if they are?

It's true that we cannot rely on others
To provide us with the never-ending
Comfort of home.

Because a home should be stable.
Grounded to the foundation upon which it was built.

But people move.
People change.
People are free.

Something I have learned in my twenty-three years
Is that home does not need to be confined
To oneself
Or to one location.

I have moved seven times in the last five years,
And I have felt that each place was home to me
While I was living
In it.

And when I venture back to these places,
Those old feelings return to the surface.

And my eyes glisten
With fondness
For what once was
And for the growth that has happened
Since I last stepped foot
There.

the garden daughter

And that's the thing.

People are homes, for a time.
And it is a beautiful thing to leave part of your heart
With them,
Even if they don't stay forever.

We leave tokens of ourselves
With each person
We meet.

Our mannerisms,
Our smile,
The way our laugh rings across
The room.

These things stay with the ones
Whom we are growing
Alongside.

And before we
Realize
What we have done,
We have built a home
Within that person.

We have made ourselves comfortable
There.

And when this home departs,
It
     hurts.

It is never easy to pack up our things
And step out
Into the cold air.

the garden daughter

To step away from the very thing
That made us feel safe.

But it is necessary
For growth.

So yes, people are homes.
We occupy space in their hearts
In the same way
They occupy space in ours.

And when it's time to move on,
We are met with those same feelings
We encountered
When we said goodbye to our childhood homes.

But this pain does not last forever.
And we are better because of it.

Know this: you are too beautiful
And unique
And extraordinary
To be forgotten.

You were home to so many,
And you always will be.

And whatever pieces of your heart
You left behind—
They will carry those pieces with them
Forever.

When the Rain Comes

I've found some form of peace
In loneliness.
Is that so bad?

I've found some quiet spaces
Where I can think
And let God
Speak.

The world isn't anxious.
Nature isn't
Rushed.

Just now,
I am sitting on the back patio
Of my childhood home.
Somewhere I never thought I would be
At this
Moment.

I am in awe of the peacefulness of nature
In the midst of the chaos
That has rooted itself
Inside my own
Little world.

A timeline of how life is supposed to go
Is a dangerous, man-made
Trap.

I think I get so sucked up
In this timeline
That I am often willing to sacrifice
Parts of myself
In order to fit within

the garden daughter

Its
Constraints.

God doesn't want it to be this way.

I am trying not to hurry.
I am trying to trust
Even though
I cannot see
What is two feet
In front of me.

I do know this:
When the rain comes,
God is preparing us.
He is watering us.
He is helping us
Grow.

He is reminding us of who we are.
Who we always have been.

And He is gently giving us
The courage
To finally
Bloom.

the garden daughter

My Grandmother's Window

A small, square frame dressed in delicate lace. White fabric
Worn down from years of sun-bathing.

The scent of an old quilt, loved deeply by time,
Tickles my nose. I bury myself deeper within its embrace.

I watch the morning sun's dance as it beams through
Cracks in that old window.
As it pours through those worn curtains,
Pooling
On the carpet, the well-loved quilt, my heart.

And beyond this window, I see it
Sparkling
Atop snow-capped trees wrapped in winter's wondrous
warmth.

I see it descend below these branches, painting my
grandmother's
Sidewalks a soft, buttery glow.

The kind of yellow only early morning earth wears.

My mind wanders as my eyes follow suit,
Back to that small window.

It urges me to chase, catch, store in my pockets.

With this ambition, I rise,
A new mind to face the coming day.

A golden hand held out gingerly for *me*.
And I take it.

So morning light and I dance together in that room

the garden daughter

Beneath my grandmother's window.

Here, I let light in, even if small,
Even if barely noticeable at first.
I let it seep into every corner of my soul.

And *you.*

I hope you chase light only to find
It chases you.

Time & Love

How do I know when I'm ready
For love?
In all honesty,
I don't think I'll ever be ready.

I don't think love has to be something
We prepare and
Plan for.
I don't think it has to be
Scheduled.

Love doesn't come when we hit a certain age,
When we get a certain job,
Or when we "have our lives together."

Whatever that means.

Because do we ever truly have it all together?
And even when we do,
The moment is fleeting.
We spend our whole lives picking up the pieces of each new mess.
But we are human enough
To make beauty out of it.

Does love wait for us?
I don't think so.
Love is other-worldly.
Love is a gift from above.
It chases us like a spring breeze on a winter day.
Unexpected,
Beautiful,
Inviting.

We either dance in that breeze

the garden daughter

Or we lock ourselves inside
And push it
Away.

I want to dance.

Love is too brave and too loud to wait
Until we are ready.
It comes in full force and wraps us up when we least expect
it.
Otherwise, it wouldn't be love.
Because love doesn't follow our rules.

I miss the feeling of new love.
I miss its timid glances,
Hands grazing against each other,
The uncertainty of a first kiss.

Time stops in these moments.
Time loves us enough to slow down
And let us
Breathe in
This new feeling.

And my whole heart yearns for it,
But I will
Wait.

This time last year,
The idea of love made me sick.
But now I have found my old self.
I have found the girl who romanticizes
Everything.

And I never want
To lose
Her.

the garden daughter

Great healing has taken place
Since this time last year.
I hope you feel the same for yourself, too.
To be able to yearn for love again
Is an indication of this
Healing.

I will find joy in this yearning
And waiting
Because it means I am finally whole enough
To feel like
Me
Again.

I choose to dance.

Old Love

I need the sun like I need air.
I need its warmth that gently strokes my skin,
Making me feel
Like me
Again.

I loved the summer with my entire
Heart.
And for the first time in a long time,
It loved me in return.

And one who has loved and been loved in return
Knows what a glorious feeling that is.

But one who has ever watched that love end,
Knows there are few things
As painful
As saying goodbye to the very person
You called home.

I have loved often and hard only to be set to the wayside.
Only to be thrown out like
Last spring's flower clippings.

And there I lie,
Wilting in the great
Wilderness
As my love's head turns
Toward the summer blooms.

But I did not need such love
When I had the warm embrace
Of the summer sun.

It felt like an old friend

the garden daughter

I had not seen in
Far too long.
It felt comfortable and familiar.
A trustworthy kind of home.

So many things were new
That summer–

Who I was now becoming
Fighting for space next to who I once was.

But I have walked this meadow before.

I recognize its blooms,
Its green grass,
The way each stem moves in the breeze.

But this time,
Something is different.
Something is better.

The blooms seem a little taller
And a little brighter.
The grass seems a resonant shade of green.

And as I travel on,
I see clearly:
It is not the meadow
That has changed.

It is *me*.

I am older and wiser,
But I am still youthful and naive.
I still long for that fairytale
Ending.

the garden daughter

But I am not yet old enough to know
Everything I should
On my own.

So for now,
I will walk alone.
I will admire the blooms as I go.

And I will be better
When summer greets me once again
As that old familiar friend.

I will be better when its sunshine
Paints my skin.

the garden daughter

If I,
And the stories the oak holds deep within his branches

Stretching,
Strong branches
Subtly shifting with the wind.
Cracked, aged bark
Reflecting the lines on my fingertips.

Leaves now painted deep hues of crimson,
Copper,
Gold,
By the tender brush of time.
Floating,
Fluttering,
Falling to the ground,
A gentle goodnight to sweet summertime.

If I sit beneath the shade of his ever-changing canopy,
If I press my ear upon his trunk,
Would I hear his tender heartbeat?

If I look,
Would I find a forlorn face?
If I lean lightly on his roots,
Would he wrap me in his ancient embrace?

My oak tree.

Standing tall in the front yard of my childhood home.
Oh, what stories his aged, wise mind must hold.

I've watched him through that small window
All the seasons through.

I've seen the clothes he wears.
The green summers,

the garden daughter

The rich falls,
The coldest winters.

And yet,
He comes back even brighter and better.

If I take a page from his book,
If I turn a new leaf,
Perhaps I would wear the changing colors of life so well.

Perhaps I, too,
Would dig deeper into the beauty
Of quiet things.

Washed Away

I remember my bare feet
Against the dirt trail
As we ran a race against the sun.

A dip in the spring.
That's what we longed for.

The sun was steadily
Saying goodbye.
She was leaving us with her
Magnificent colors;
Her warm welcome to the moon.

But we made it to the spring.

And I won't soon forget
The rush I felt
As my whole body was washed by the fresh, frigid water.

It washed away every
Heartbreak
I had been wearing on my face.

Yes, it washed it all
Away.

And I am reminded of this:
The journey to healing is a long one.

It is as long as that dirt
Trail
My bare feet once
Ran upon.

But I also know this:

the garden daughter

The spring washed
It all
Away
In one quick
Move.

Yes, in this way,
I know
We have the strength
To wake up and start over.

To be brand new.

Remembering the Important Stories

Some memories are so
Distant,
We often forget they even
Existed.

But all it takes
Is a sentence
Or a song
Or a scent
To bring them flooding back.

All it takes is one of these simple things,
And suddenly
We are transported.

And while I have an abundance of good memories,
There are a few I do not wish
To see again.

But I am prepared for when
They hop to the surface.
For it is not a matter of if,
But
    when.

We all have things we wish to
Forget.
But we learn from those things.

They lead us to the person we are
Becoming.
Perhaps a person we have not met
Yet.

So yes,

the garden daughter

While I have memories that
Make my eyes burn
And my heart ache,
I also have memories that
Remind me
Of the best days.

In spite of the pain,
There is still hope in what is
Left to live.

There are still books to read
And songs to play
And places I have not yet visited.

There are still people I need
To forgive.

So continue on.
Keep reading your story.
And where you find the bad memories
Lurking,
Remind yourself that every new day
Is an opportunity
For newer,
Better stories.

And I hope you will tell yours.

Because the best stories are lined with
Hope,
And forgiveness,
And love.

These stories, yes—
They exist
In each of us.

the garden daughter

Dive

I fell out of love
Then almost fell
Back in.
One heart broken twice
In less than
A year.

But I learned that I am far too willing
To dive right in.

I am far too eager
To forget myself
And jump into the deep end.

Headfirst,
Hands ahead of me,
No vision of what lies underneath.

But I did not make the same mistake twice.

I peered over the edge of the boat
And caught my reflection
In the water as still
As glass.

Instead of asking, "Who are you?"
I smiled
And said,
"We are slowly becoming who we are meant to be."

That summer I found myself.
Or at least,
A version of me.

Because life is a never-ending
Journey
Of finding who we

the garden daughter

Want to be.
And I don't think we ever truly find that person,
Because if we did,
What good is the chase?

What fun is the dense wood,
The forest that is less than inviting
That calls to us and says,
"I know you don't want to go this way,
But you must.
I promise
There is a meadow
Inside of me."

And the adventurer in us all,
(Because it exists in each of us),
Takes the first small step
On the path.

And even though
We do not know
What lies ahead,
We take the journey anyway.

We collect different versions of ourselves
As we go.

Some we like more than others.

Some are more authentic.
Some make us feel
More like
Who we think we ought to be.

Some are simply a combination
Of those who have traveled alongside us
For this leg
Of the journey.

the garden daughter

The ones who influenced us,
Affected us,
Impacted who
We were growing to be.

And sometimes we are not
Strong enough
To decipher which one we truly are,
So we lean on those other weary travelers
To make us feel whole.

But we are often left empty,
And they often leave,
And we are left alone yet again
On the dark,
Dense trail.

And it is here where we find ourselves.
It is here where we discover
Who we want to be.

But take caution
As you travel.

The dark,
Deep end
Often seems mysterious and
Inviting.

But before you dive
In,
Make sure that you
Have healed.

Yes,
Before you dive in,
I beg you,
Make sure
You are ready.

Heartbreak

There is hope in pain and there is
Discovery
As well as
Inspiration.

There are new horizons.
New people,
New heartbreaks.
Yes, plenty more heartbreaks,
Unfortunately.

But at the end of every
Road,
There remains
You.

And you must love who you are.

Because the truth is that no one
Can complete you.
You are not half of a person
Waiting
To meet your other half
Who fits you
Just right.

You are whole as you are,
And anything else is simply an
Addition.

You must not waste your
Time
On the ones who make you feel
Less
Than whole.

the garden daughter

You are
Interesting,
Unique,
Smart,
Funny,
Beautiful.

You must learn this on your own
And you must love your life
As it is
Right now.

Love where God has placed you
Right now.
See the good in where your feet are
Planted.

Things are the way they are for a
Reason.

And just as you did not understand then,
And now you do;
Soon you will understand this heartache,
Too.

Summer Snapshot

I remember yearning
For what I have now.

For comforting friendships,
Silence interrupted,
Their laughter, the warmest sound.

I pause in these moments.
I look around.

I marvel at the way
The world works.
How hope, & goodness, & love
Abound.

Some may capture this
In photographs,
But I try to use words.

I tell you that
It is summer,
It is warm,
There is an evening glow.

The cicadas sing,
The docks on the lake are creaking.

I take a mental image
And look back on it
Fondly.

Dancing with Flowers

I was drawn back home after the world turned
Upside down.

I was reluctant at first.

My mother told me I was
Welcome
At any time.

She said I could pack up my
Apartment
And move back
For the summer
If I desired.

Eventually,
My apartment became too stuffy
To even think straight.

I was restless and
Eager
For the outdoors.
For things I hadn't felt in a while.

So I packed my bags and drove home.

I spent more time outside in the greenhouse
Than I did in the actual house
That summer.

I helped my father move
Trays of flowers
From within the plastic
Walls.

the garden daughter

The greenhouses had grown
Much too hot for the flowers
Mid-summertime.

They wanted what they could not have.
What the sun had claimed as her own.

They were able to
Breathe
Again
After they had been set
Free.

The sunlight bathed their beautiful faces
With a warm,
Golden light,
And I couldn't help but get a little
Teary-eyed
Thinking about how I too
Had finally been set free
And given room
To breathe.

I too was letting the sunshine wrap me
In its
Warmth.

I was letting it
Bring me
Back
To me.

Seems like everyone my age
Believes that going away to school
Is freedom.

But for me,

Freedom is found in
Coming home.

It's giving my mind something
Tangible
To hold on to.

The feeling roots itself deep
Into my
Bones.

And because of the bliss
That comes with this
Safe,
Stable feeling,
I can't help but believe in a
Second chance.

Yes,
Because of this feeling,
I can't help but ask the flowers
If they would like
To dance.

Weary Travelers

And maybe I'm trying too hard to fit
Into too many spaces.

But I feel my heart pulled in a million
Different directions
And I can't quite decipher
Which direction
Calls to me.

I believe it takes courage to embark on the journey.

But take caution as you travel,
Because it is unbelievable the ways in which you will sacrifice
Yourself
In order to fit
Into the mold
Of someone else's
Story.

If no one tells you this today,
Please remember that you are worth far too much
To simply be
A background character
In another's plot.

No, you are real and vulnerable and
Complex,
And you should not shrink yourself down
To fit between the lines of the pages of a
Book
That was not written
For you.

When life gets tough,
It can define who a person is and could be.

But endurance is a friend to the broken and the
Weary,
Reminding you to never let heartbreak leave you
Bitter.

Don't let it close you off
To the life
That you are meant
To lead.

It's true that you can't have the rainbow without the storm,
And let that remind you
That one person's rejection
Only pushes you
One step closer
To the ray of colors you
Long for.

And your story has so much
Potential
To end happily,
With family and memorable days
Forevermore.

But in the meantime,
While the storm rages on
And the paths don't make sense,
Do the brave thing
And embrace the rain like the flowers in the spring.

Do the brave thing and bloom here
Now
In this chapter,
Anyway.

the garden daughter

the garden daughter

perennial

the garden daughter

the garden daughter

Hope has been a near and dear friend to me recently. She's sitting with me now at a coffee shop, which feels like my second home lately. It's where I am sitting now, writing these words. I am convinced she has been a near and dear friend my entire life, but I am only now old enough to truly recognize her presence—the way it takes shape in all forms, whether in the good or the bad. She is always there, embracing me, walking with me, whispering words of encouragement alongside me.

We laugh together, because I feel like I have come full circle. I feel as though, in many ways, I am starting all over again. I am starting with new seeds—waiting eagerly for a new garden to bloom. I am preparing to start a new job, I am living in a new home, I am writing a book… It is just a gentle reminder to me that we will never stop beginning again. That we will never stop believing and creating new things.

I feel like I finally understand that I am always right where I am meant to be. I have watched God write my story—I have seen His hand in every chapter, in every dark place, in every joyous place. I am here. And I have dreams for the future. But right now I am here, and I am learning to slow down and continuously learn to love exactly where I am. Because God is here, and my friend Hope is here, and there is beauty all around me. And those things seem to never leave, no matter how hard the season may be.

I love these poems with my whole heart. This section contains some of my oldest and newest poems—you may be able to spot the difference as you read. But before you dive in, I believe it is important that you understand what a perennial flower is—what that definition actually means. A perennial is a flower that blooms time and time again. But what's interesting is that the above-ground portion of the plant dies in the winter with the freezing temperatures. However, the base and roots of the plant remain intact and regrow and bloom each spring.

I just think that is one of the most beautiful things— that despite the freezing cold, these flowers press on and choose to bloom again anyway. They make it through the cold because they remember what the sun feels like. They choose to keep going because they know they will experience that warmth again like they did last season.

    I pray that, like the other sections of this book, Hope will grip your hand tightly as you read. Despite whatever season of your life you're living in, or what whirlwind of emotions you may be feeling; I pray you will accept Hope's offered hand, that you will pause with her in the midst of the chaos, that you will let her remind you of the beautiful things in your life that are worth experiencing. There are so many things that make your life worth living.

Two Pines

I have always loved the trees.

I admire their strength,
The way their branches
Dance
In the breeze.

As a young girl,
I spent hours
Searching for the right trees
To climb.

I wanted to get as close as I could
To the top.
I wanted to reach for the
Summer sun.
To call it mine.

There were two trees
In our yard
That I particularly loved
Best.

I made a fort in between
Where they were growing
Side by side–
My own personal
Nest.

I let my imagination run wild
Within the branches of those
Two pine trees.

I wrote books that I would
Never publish.
Silly tales and
Short stories.

the garden daughter

My dreams started
Within the branches of
Those pines.

But lightning struck,
And my beautiful trees were
Gone.
The two
Magnificent pillars
That felt like
Mine.

For a while,
I felt that my creativity
Had died with
Them.

But years later,
I realized that it just needed
A new space to
Grow.
I needed trees with new
Stems.

So my mother put up a
Hammock
Where those trees once
Swayed.

And I spent hours in the same
Spot
As a teenager–
But this time with the
Absence of
Shade.

I read countless books
In that hammock.
I wrote a few more

the garden daughter

Short stories,
Too.

And I was reminded that
The things in our hearts
Never truly die.

They just look for
New places
To reside.

For me,
That space was the
Beautiful land
Between my two
Noble friends.

My two pine trees.

And every time
I return to that home,
I hear their whispers

In the soft breeze.

Observations From a Fallen Tree

Perched on a fallen tree, feet dangling above clear waters,
I watch.

As leaves cascade softly, silently grazing the earth without a sound.

Why do we call it falling?

To me, it looks like floating into place, unafraid.

The creek moves along unceasingly, accepting each
Bend and curve, each
Dip in depth or
Shallow resurfacing.

It flickers across sun-kissed river stones,
Like soft candle light on cold autumn nights.

A bird glides overhead.
Circling, observing,
Living.

I, too, long for this.
To slip smoothly from branches that bind me.
To land gently atop the brook and
Float, wherever
He may lead me.

Wonder, Wonder, Wonder

At 30,000 feet, I marvel.
When did blue look so tangible? Like I might reach out and
Hold it in my hands, taking pieces of floating clouds with me.
To be human up here, to soar higher than the birds.
How did I ever let fear convince me this was not
Wonder, wonder, wonder?

And when again my feet meet the earth,
I am met with a new hue of blue.
Tell me, when did it get so vibrant, so lively, *so warm?*

The rhythmic lapping of waves against the shore.
It slows my internal clock, my breath, my heart.
I stare.
Who could ever peel their eyes away from this
Wonder, wonder, wonder?

The next moment, I converse with complete strangers.
All they want is to know my story.
Where are you from? What do you do? Who do you love?
When did I forget that storytelling has always been in our hearts?
When did I forget that we're all chasing
Wonder, wonder, wonder?

And when I close my eyes to sleep at night,
I can't seem to keep them shut.
Because wonder, when you let it in, shines bright as summer sun.

Tell me, who is fear?
I can't seem to remember his name.

I open my eyes and all I see is
Wonder, wonder, wonder.

Thyme

"Never Enough Thyme"
This short sentiment is painted
In white letters
Against a dark green,
Faded wood
Backdrop.

It hangs in my mother's shop,
Surrounded by plants and herbs
Of all kinds.

But what do I know about thyme?
I know it is sweet
And spicy
To the nose.

But to my nose,
Sweet reigns supreme.

I bend down over the plant
And breathe in its aroma.

A flood of memories
Crash through the dam
I had built to hide them all deep
Inside me.

And I am left
Reflecting.

Of all the seasons in the year,
It seems there is never enough time
In the summer.

Never enough time
To do all the adventurous things

the garden daughter

We said we would do when it began.

Never enough time
To fall in love.

Never enough time
To say all the words
We need to say
To those whose presence is only felt
In the summertime.

Time,
Just like thyme,
Can be both sweet and spicy.

But in my mind,
I try to view it as mostly
Sweet.

Time is sweet when we slow down and breathe in the moment.

We get into trouble when we try to rush it.
When we try to fast forward
To the season
We long
To be living in.

Time is independent,
And time knows what's best.
When we manipulate her,
We are met with her
Spices.

Because we cannot control time.
We must flow along
With where she leads us.

An Ode to Love Lost and Found Again

Those two windows, morning light stretching inside.
Those four walls, hugging me in a warm embrace.
The tears begging to trickle, to rush forth, but I hold them tight.
                    I've seen better days.

My childhood bedroom, a place I loved for years.
A place I admire visiting, but with no intention to stay.
Never had I imagined to be back here.
                    I've seen better days.

Oh, if I could go back and hug that girl from years ago.
I would tell her of the beauty that awaits.
I would tell her that God sees her, that He knows.
                    I've seen better days.

Four years later, I am back in that tiny room.
And now, my mom is here, zipping me into my dress on my wedding day.
And I think of that girl I used to know, who cried here, who did not know all she was meant to.
                    Yes, I had seen better days.

But how blessed am I to finally be living in them.

Say Yes

The morning light was peeking
Through
The thin curtains
Of that tiny bedroom.

And as I basked in its
Warmth,
I was reminded of His mercies
That are made new
Every morning.

I was reminded that every
Yes
I have ever said to God
Has led me to this
Moment.

Every yes I have ever said to God,
Even the ones that hurt,
Even the times I would have rather said
No.
Yes, even those.

Every yes I have ever said to God
Has come back to me
In full
Bloom.

New Endings

To love
Is to immerse yourself
In deep water.

There,
Beneath the surface,
One is never sure of when
The time
Is
Right.

And yet,
I swim deeper.
I swim as far as my dreams
Will take me.

But eventually,
You must come up for air.

You must breathe.

And when I land on the surface,
And when my legs are able,
I do my best to follow
The right path
Home.

But is the right path really mine?

I want the path lined with sunflowers.
I want the path where empathy is as present as the summer sun
That warms my skin.

I fear I am always met
With melancholy

the garden daughter

Endings.

But I am encouraged by the sunflowers
Who thrive in the deep water.
Who thrive when the rain pours.

So I will craft my own ending.
I will take charge of my
Story.
And it will be lined
With endless
Hope.

the garden daughter

Daffodils

The first sign of spring–
That beautiful flower
Peeking through
The snow.

That yellow color
Is the first flower
Of the season.
And it means much more
To me
Than it will ever
Know.

It begins its journey in October.
Just a small seed growing
In the earth.
And it grows strong
And tall–
A symbol of
Rebirth.

It reminds me that
Warmer days are
Ahead.

It reminds me that
There is beauty
In growth.

It reminds me to
Persevere–
To keep growing through
The winter cold.

And when I see that

the garden daughter

Yellow flower,
I am reminded that the sun is once again
Mine.

And it begs me to remember:
The most beautiful things
Take time.

the garden daughter

It's the First Day of Spring, So

Let me tell you about the way the
Flowers sang to me yesterday.
It was small and timid and beautiful.

Much like joy sounds when it seems far away.

But then I knelt down;
I let myself go into the valley.

There, I touched their petals gently.
I poured water on their soil.

All they needed was an observant,
Wonder-filled eye
To care for them
Before they displayed beauty in all its glory.

And I wonder,
How often have you ignored joy's whispers?

When was the last time you watered that small seed in your heart?

V Road

I'm driving down that road
You have always loved.
You know the one;
It's the long way home.

Her bends and twists are
Jarring.
And I know that one who is
Unfamiliar
With the way she dances
May not be prepared for her surprising
Steps.

But you and I,
We've spent our whole lives
Learning each of her
Tricks.
In eighteen years,
She hasn't fooled us yet.

And seeing as this road is the one
Familiar
Thing from the past,
I don't think she ever
Will.

We've spent nearly our entire
Lives
Leaning into her movements.
So much so that her turns
Almost feel
Like a lullaby.

Fall is quietly peeking
Behind the corner.
She's always timid at first,
But she can't help but show
Little bits of her beauty

the garden daughter

On that old road.

Splashes of color pop
Orange,
Red,
And brown
In the midst of the sea
Of never-ending green.

The trees sway with the
Wind.
The sunlight trickles in
Through the spaces
In between
The leaves.

It dances on the
Pavement.
Shadows creating nature's own
Sheet music.

Everything on this road seems to exist
In perfect
Harmony.

Each member seems to be
Dancing
To the very same tune.

After years of being lost,
And years of traveling down
Other roads,
I lost my sense of that lyrical song.

But now it seems
I can hear the music
Once again.
That no matter how far I travel,
I am never too
Far gone.

To Gentle Souls: A Butterfly's Song

Butterfly wings flutter earnestly,
A small speck of sunset colors against the
Vibrant shade of green leaves nestled in towering trees.

Gentle,
Delicate wings,
Yet
Strong enough to traverse the blue skies
And land softly
Atop long-awaited petals.

And you,
Catching a glimmer of this quaint creature,
Relish in this flicker of a peaceful song
Written by nature;
Slowing your pace
As you pay mind to the small,
Simple things.

You are not too gentle.

With that softness that rests at the edges of your eyes,
With those flower
Petals
Pressed along the lining of your heart, a soft spot.

Do not keep that gentle heart cocooned inside.

Let it burst forth,
Painting rose petals on the ends of your sleeves.
Let it sing a new, soft-spoken melody.

For the world would be lacking beauty if those butterflies
Never woke and
Took flight;

the garden daughter

If they never trusted their soft wings.

You, too, can wear that gentle heart on your sleeve.

Let it brush gracefully against weary souls it was created to meet.

Bloom

It is easy
To allow certain seeds
To take root in our hearts.

Seeds of
Bitterness,
Envy,
Defeat.

They sprout in our souls and they bloom
On our faces,
In our words,
Our interactions,
Our relationships.

I am begging you.

Plant seeds of
Kindness,
Hope,
And love
Instead.

Let those seeds take root
Deep inside
You.
Let them sprout in your soul.

And when people ask what has
Changed,
Why your face has a new
Glow,
Tell them of the seeds you nurture
Inside of you.
Show them the beauty of the

the garden daughter

Blooming
In your life.
In every aspect of it.

And maybe,
Just maybe,
We can spread these seeds
Like the most abundant
Weeds.

And maybe,
Just maybe,
We'll see that
Weeds
Can be
Flowers
Too.

To the Writer and Artist / To Being Human

My words, held captive,
Trapped in tight crevices,
Stripped of sunlight.
Reaching,
      Reaching,
           Reaching,
Gasping for air.

They dance along the front of my brain,
Lingering
At the tip of my tongue.
My mind refusing to let them take shape.

Neglecting them,
Keeping them hidden,
An arm's length away from my pen and page.

Why do I lock my creativity into these tight boxes?

When my Creator threw limitations and
Boxes and
Rules to the wayside when
He made me.

When He made *you*.

Yes, He let every wild thought
Burst forth, unafraid, a sense of
Urgency and wonder and glory
Filling,
Illuminating,
A once dark and empty space.

Just look at what He has done.

the garden daughter

Wildflowers in parades of colors, standing tall,
Saluting the sun.
Birds taking flight,
Awakening the world with their loveliest,
Liveliest,
Concert.
A sacred song.

Just look at how the wind blows,
Howling,
Shaking tallest treetops as it invites them to
Dance,
       Dance,
              Dance,

To let loose and feel the strength of that breeze,
How it wildly whips their leaves,
Their hair.
Just look at the wonders our Creator has made and
Loved.

What He called *good*.

Look at you.

There are oceans in your eyes,
Tree trunk lines on your fingertips.

There is power in your legs,
Your arms,
Sunshine radiating off your face.

He did not trap creativity inside a box
When He made you.
He did not snuff out its light.

And you, too, were born to create in this way.

To unashamedly spread beauty and sing loudly of His love
Everywhere you go.

Now, set forth,
Do the good work.
Love the Lord and
Love people.

Break down the edges of that box,
Let His love ripple through you.
Let it pour out your heart and into your words,
Painting
This broken world.

Crafting Bouquets of Ordinary Things

When I feel too small or
plain or
afraid I should be doing
grander things,

I feel the Lord cup my cheek and shift my gaze.

My eyes wander, then, to ordinary things.

Like tiny droplets of rain
>*Cascading*
>>along flower petals
after hot summer days.

Or small living rooms
>*bursting*
>>at the seams with laughter and
light and
warmth,
as the feeling of home blooms in our hearts.

Or the stillness of trees.
The way they don't chase praise but
>*remain rooted*
>>in the One
Who is greater.

So I take these moments—
I pluck them like flowers.
I arrange them and
marvel at their beauty when placed together in this way.

The Lord looks at me then, as if to say:
"I hope you craft bouquets
of *wonderful,*
>*ordinary things.*"

the garden daughter

the garden daughter

the garden daughter

enjoy the blooms

the garden daughter

The Garden Daughter
A longing and a lesson from weeds and flowering things

I. Rose

I went out to pick roses from my mother's garden when I was a little girl.
Perhaps if I held one in my hand, eye-catching beauty would spread to my face.
Perhaps if I kneeled down and pressed my nose against its gentle petals, sweet scents and striking color would seep deeply into me.

My rose-colored glasses didn't see the thorns.

I went out to pick roses from my mother's garden when I was a little girl.
But I came back with pricked skin and a longing to be lovely.

II. Daisy

"He loves me, he loves me not" as I pluck daisy petals.
My heart, twisting at its fateful end.
Why does the dismantling of a flower carry such weight?
Why am I left seated in my self-induced massacre?

A collage of petals spread all around me.

"He loves me, he loves me not" as I pluck daisy petals.
As I am left with scattered beauty and a single stem.

III. Moonflower

I took a walk in the greenhouse one night as a teen.
In search, or insomnia; perhaps both.
But there, crawling up the trellises in spirals like my thoughts, a foreign thing.

the garden daughter

There, a flower bathed in moonlight; its bright, white petals illuminating the whole space.

There, at seventeen, quiet beauty was starting to make sense to me.

I took a walk in the greenhouse one night as a teen.
And I came back with hidden flowers and an inkling of what it meant to be sought after.

IV. Gomphrena

The gomphrena healed me at twenty-three.
Holding its tender roots, placing it gently in the earth.
Here, blooming tall among the most well-known flowers.
Here, stealing the show, face reaching for the sun.

Stem towering, as magnificent and enchanting as ancient trees.

The gomphrena healed me at twenty-three.
And as I take a step back to admire my garden, I hear it whisper, "You, too, are worthy of space."

V. Weeds and Wildflowers

"Weeds will grow whether they are wanted or not." My father says to me.
My twenty-six year old hands pick them among flowers of every color.
Crafting bouquets of unexpected things;
Crafting bundles of beauty I am only now wise enough to understand.
Clovers, dandelions, chicory, periwinkle.

"Weeds will grow whether they are wanted or not." My father says to me.
So with wildflowers pressed against my heart, I grow.

ACKNOWLEDGEMENTS

This book is a tangible copy of a dream come true. I want to thank you first, as a reader, for picking up this book and giving it a chance. For spending your time reading it, for letting it have a home on your bookshelf. It means everything to me and more.

Thank you, Elizabeth Hughes and Caitlyn Spencer, for your incredible support throughout the entire process. Your encouragement kept me going every step of the way. You both believed in me as a writer, and for the first time in my life I actually felt like one. I don't know how to fully express how thankful I am for you both.

Thank you to my friends who continuously encourage my dreams. Having you all by my side, cheering me on, makes my heart swell with unfathomable joy. I have prayed and prayed for friends like you, and I am so thankful every day that God's answer to that prayer was you. I just love you guys so much.

To my family–there are no words. You are the ones who have been there since the very beginning–since that little girl was just six years old and she told you she wanted to write a book one day. Thank you for sharing every poem, for talking about my book with your friends, and for always offering up words of encouragement. You were my very first readers, and you continue to be the most loyal. I am so thankful to have a family that encourages all creative dreams, no matter how unrealistic they may be. You paint the earth with bright colors everywhere you go. There is simply no one like you.

Thank you to my husband, Bengt, for absolutely everything. I could write about you for pages and pages and pages. For your endless support, for reading everything I write, for sharing every poem I post, for reminding me that it isn't stupid or ridiculous to chase the dreams I have. For being creative, for inspiring me, for showing me that love exists in ways I have never experienced before. I love you and adore you and could not picture my life without you.

Lastly, I would like to thank the editors of the

following publications in which these poems previously appeared.

Vessels of Light Literary Journal: "At the Beach"; "To the Writer and Artist / To Being Human"

The Way Back to Ourselves Literary Journal: "If I,"

The Wondrous Nature of Being Alive, an anthology by Twenty Hills Publishing: "To the Earthworm's Work"; "To Gentle Souls: A Butterfly's Song"

Prosetrics: "My Grandmother's Window"

the garden daughter

Taylor Blayse is a wife, writer, and greenhouse manager for her family's business, The Garden Party. She holds a B.A. in both music and English from the University of Missouri. In her writing, Taylor loves to explore themes of hope, whimsy, wonder, and childlike faith. Her writing has been published at Calla Press, The Way Back to Ourselves, Humana Obscura, Twenty Hills, Prosetrics, and others. When she isn't writing, she can be found reading, spending time with friends, gardening, wandering around bookstores, and enjoying the outdoors. To read more of her poetry and fiction, visit her substack or instagram: @taylorblayse.

www.ingramcontent.com/pod-product-compliance
Lightning Source LLC
Chambersburg PA
CBHW070144080526
44586CB00015B/1828